Motherhood Is

Stranger Than Fiction

mary chambers

INTERVARSITY PRESS
DOWNERS GROVE, ILLINOIS 60515

©1995 by Mary Chambers

InterVarsity Press® is the book-publishing division of InterVarsity Christian Fellowship®, a student movement active on campus at hundreds of universities, colleges and schools of nursing in the United States of America, and a member movement of the International Fellowship of Evangelical Students. For information about local and regional activities, write Public Relations Dept., InterVarsity Christian Fellowship, 6400 Schroeder Rd., P.O. Box 7895, Madison, WI 53707-7895.

Cover illustration: Mary Chambers

ISBN 0-8308-1603-8

Printed in the United States of America ∞

Library of Congress Cataloging-in-Publication Data has been requested.

17   16   15   14   13   12   11   10   9   8   7   6   5   4   3   2   1
09   08   07   06   05   04   03   02   01   00   99   98   97   96   95

To my husband, Tim,
who made me what I am today,
a happy mother of six,
and to my mom, Betty Mouton,
who baby-sat five of them for a month
so I could finish this book.

Introduction

I am expecting my sixth child. Any mom can tell you how ironic it is to begin motherhood by "expecting," because actually it means you will *never* know what to expect ever again. If you expect to leave on vacation, your kids will come down with chickenpox. If you expect to wear your red blouse to church, the baby will throw up on it. If you expect to sit down and do a book of cartoons on motherhood, you will get pregnant and spend the next three months either in bed or in the bathroom. At least that's what happened to me.

Long-suffering editors can't wait forever, though. So at the eleventh hour I packed up the kids and sent them to my mom's for a month. (See, I bet she wasn't expecting that.) Some day I'll tell this baby about all those long quiet days alone at my desk with my wondrous jumping belly and how glad I was of his company. This is probably not the last time he will complicate my plans. I hope not. I'm expecting it.

"Oh, thank goodness! You're just here to *rob* us! I was afraid you might be my daughter's new boyfriend!"

Researchers now suggest that women's pathological obsession with their weight and dissatisfaction with their appearance can be traced to the way they were dressed as infants.

"Look at me when I'm talking to you! Maybe you think I'm standing up here for my health. Maybe you think I just like to hear myself talk."

"Mother . . . please tell me this isn't you in these hideous bell-bottoms."

"Yeah, yeah, I know . . . Jimmy Morris gets straight A's, Joel McPeak doesn't read comics during church and James Marcum practices his piano without being reminded. By the way . . . did you know that Phillip Bailey's mom bakes all their bread, runs a $60,000-a-year business from their home and can still fit into her wedding dress?"

"What's the 'mother's special'? Anything that table over there doesn't eat."

"No, you can't count eating leftovers as your history project."

"I invited four families home for dinner and none could make it.
I got to be hospitable without even cooking!"

YOU KNOW YOU'RE A MOTHER WHEN...
WAIT! DON'T GO!
YOU'RE SO STARVED FOR ADULT CONVERSATION YOU TRY TO KEEP TELEMARKETERS ON THE LINE.
chambers

"Awwww . . . how long till she's old enough to wash dishes?"

"Yes, Ma'am. I'm here to investigate a report of plant abuse."

"It says right here on the box—up to 16 lbs. It can't be near that full!"

"Uh oh. If we don't convince her she looks great—and *fast*—we'll all be eating cottage cheese for months!"

"Look, *I* know it's just scribbles and *you* know it's just scribbles, but for some odd reason my mom will pretend she can read it!"

"O.K., Sweeties. You're all going to need to go naked for just à day or two till Mommy catches up with the laundry."

"Mother, this is my friend James. His mom said he could spend the summer with us if it's okay with you."

"Shh! Honey, the Bible says if a woman has questions, she should wait
and ask her husband at home."

"They threw out me *and* my imaginary friend . . . but my imaginary friend is going right back in!"

"Were you pretty when Daddy asked you to marry him?"

"Hey! I saw your lips move!"

"Now remember—don't tell Mom that I cut our hair."

"If Jesus is still alive, what's all this about his holy ghost?"

"My goodness! Little Josh has grown at least six inches since I saw you last!"

"I hope you don't take this as a personal attack on your parenting skills . . . but I've been having trouble with your daughter."

"Hey! I read this book you didn't think I should *three* times and I couldn't find anything bad in it!"

"Mom! William's gonna wish something mean!"

Damocles as a child

"I can't really talk right now . . . You-know-who is listening in."

"Even *I* could've told you getting Mom vacuum cleaner bags for Valentine's Day was a mistake."

Suzette had always suspected this . . .

"Hey, Mom! I want to be _him_ for Halloween!"

"I really do appreciate your interest and participation in Robbie's discipline, dear, but perhaps a simple 'chew with your mouth closed, please' would suffice."

"Rats! My blanket's in the wash and I've got to get by with this cheap loaner."

"Oh, quit 'cher whining. If I don't take pictures you might forget how much fun we're having."

"Home schooling does have its disadvantages. Have you noticed that they're picking up our bad habits faster?"

"Trick or treat! I have five kids but they couldn't make it tonight."

He had successfully negotiated peace between Egypt and Israel and mediated disagreements in Korea and Haiti, but he was stumped when it came to the Putnam boys.

"Look, Mom! He's going to have a baby too!"

"Don't be in any rush to grow up, kiddo. I just found out that when you get to be my age, they don't give treats for going to the bathroom anymore."

"He left diapers in the toilet for *me* to rinse out, your honor."

"So how's weaning going?"

"It's only for three or four years . . ."

"Oh, Honey, it was awful! I dreamed I was a mother!"

"Wait, Mom! You can't spank a sister in Christ!"

"My sister's getting married and she said birds can't eat rice so I'm gonna throw worms."

"I finally got that button sewn back on your favorite cookie monster suit!"

"It is *not* daycare, Mother, it's Sunday school, and *no*, I don't feel guilty."

"Mommies can have cookies any time they want because there's nobody here big enough to stop us."

The final straw came the day Elaina got her new driver's license . . . and it read "Elise and Ethan's mom."

"Well, what if we held you up to the stove?"

"Yes, I really am Mother's little helper. Like when we saw you guys drive up I helped her gather up all the junk in here and hide it in the dryer."

"You've been in here for 2 hours, you've used over $3.00 worth of bubble bath and all the shampoo. You've dissolved 2 cakes of soap, soaked the floor, the ceiling, half the towels and steamed the wallpaper off the walls . . . and you're dirtier than when you started."

"See, Mom? He's eating it . . . I just told him it's the stuff from the ashtrays at the bus station."

"No, she doesn't fish . . . I think they're swapping birth stories."

"Boy! I've been standing here in these shoes so long I'm getting a blister . . . Look!"

"Sweetheart, counting sheep *won't* make you sleepy if you have to keep coming in to ask me what number comes next."

"The way I see it, if you know you're lying and God knows you're lying, isn't that the same thing as telling the truth?"

"Hey, I'm watching Alex and you're right, the ankle weights really do slow him down."

Recent OSHA regulations provide stiff penalties for mothers carrying diaper bags heavier than the accompanying baby.

"Well, she's been working with a personal trainer three times a week, but it's really cutting into her studies and I'm afraid it could jeopardize her chances of getting into the gifted program at Kiddie Kollege."

"So what's my motivation in this scene?"

"I'd better not—my mom would kill me."

"Ooookay. That's enough. From now on all questions must be submitted in writing."

"Whoa, now! I'm not sure that's scriptural without an interpreter."

"I used to hate running, but I think I just associated it with trying to get a toddler to the bathroom in time at a mall."

"Eeewww! *Cured* ham? What did it have?"

"My mom makes all the little decisions and if there are ever any big decisions, my dad will make them."

"You realize, of course, that if she ever gets a cordless phone we're done for."

"Shhh! If you go 'round to Daddy's side, I'll let you watch Barney videos *all day* tomorrow!"

"Oh, Mother! What an *adorable* outfit! May I *please* borrow it if I promise not to sweat in it?"

The reason this book took so long to complete

Words to Know Before You Read

basketball

catch

chase

dance

dive

ducks

shape

stretch

swim

walk

www.rourkeeducationalmedia.com

Edited by Luana Mitten
Illustrated by John Reasoner
Art Direction and Page Layout by Renee Brady

Scan for Related Titles
and Teacher Resources

Library of Congress PCN Data

Buff Ducks / Precious McKenzie
ISBN 978-1-61810-171-6 (hard cover) (alk. paper)
ISBN 978-1-61810-304-8 (soft cover)
ISBN 978-1-61810-426-7 (eBook)
Library of Congress Control Number: 2012936763

Also Available as:

Rourke Educational Media
Printed in the United States of America,
North Mankato, Minnesota

rourkeeducationalmedia.com

customerservice@rourkeeducationalmedia.com • PO Box 643328 Vero Beach, Florida 32964

Buff Ducks

By Precious McKenzie

Illustrated by John Reasoner

Ducks get in shape.

Ducks stretch. Ducks bend.

5

Ducks walk.

Ducks waddle.
Ducks run.

Ducks dive. Ducks float.
Ducks swim.

Ducks splash.

11

Ducks shimmy. Ducks shake. Ducks dance.

Ducks dash.

14

Ducks chase.
Ducks tag.

Ducks catch.
Ducks throw.

Ducks play basketball.

18

19

Buff ducks!

21

After Reading Activities

You and the Story...

What did the ducks do before they exercised?
How many different activities did the ducks do to stay in shape?
Do you like to exercise?
What activities do you like to do to stay healthy?

Words You Know Now...

Can you find a word with a short u sound like in the word pup?
Can you find a word with a long a sound like in the word cape?

basketball	ducks
catch	shape
chase	stretch
dance	swim
dive	walk

You Could...Act Out Buff Ducks at Your House or School

- Ask a friend to act out the story with you.

- Work together to make duck masks and wings.

- Decide which duck each person will be during the show.

- Gather together to make props.

- Practice your play.

- Invite your friends and family to see your play.

About the Author

Precious McKenzie loves to write funny stories about animals. Precious lives with her husband and three children in Montana. She likes to go for walks and watch the ducks play.

Meet The Author!
www.meetREMauthors.com

About the Illustrator

John Reasoner has loved to draw ever since he was a little kid. He lives in Colorado Springs with his fiance and two dogs, Bumble and Wiggum. He gets his inspiration from walking his dogs through the local parks and playing with his niece and nephew. When not illustrating, John can be found playing his favorite video games!